THIS
WALKER BOOK
BELONGS TO:

hey nonny h

a la la la la la

Poo poo pi d

a la la la la la

a la. Whack

ooom, sh-bo

a la la la la

billy. La la la

la la la la la

oo. La la la la la

la la la la la

a doo. La la La la la

om. La la la

a la la la

a collection of
CONCRETE POEMS

selected by PAUL B. JANECZKO

illustrated by CHRIS RASCHKA

A
POKE
IN   THE
I

```
P A U L J A N E C Z K O
P A U L J A N E C H H K O O
P A U L J A A E C H H K O O
P A U I J A A E C H H K O O
P A U I J A A E C H H K A
P H U I J A A E C H H K A A
P H U I J R A E C H H K A A
C H U I J R A E C H K A A
C H U I J R A S C H K A A
C H U I J R A S C H K A A
C H R I J R A S C H K A
C H R I J R A S C H K A
C H R I S R A S C H K A
```

WALKER BOOKS
AND SUBSIDIARIES
LONDON • BOSTON • SYDNEY • AUCKLAND

First published 2001 by Walker Books Ltd
87 Vauxhall Walk, London SE11 5HJ

This edition published 2005

2 4 6 8 10 9 7 5 3 1

The right of Chris Raschka to be identified as
illustrator of this work has been asserted by him in
accordance with the Copyright, Designs and Patents Act 1988

This book has been typeset in Plantin, Futura, Avant Garde and Officina Serif
The illustrations were done in watercolour, ink and torn paper

Printed in China

British Library Cataloguing in Publication Data:
a catalogue record for this book is available
from the British Library

ISBN 0-7445-8940-1

www.walkerbooks.co.uk

To the memory of my father,
Frank Janeczko (1914–2000)
This one's for you, Pop.
Thanks for everything.
P. B. J.

To Richard Foster
C. R.

TABLE
OF
CONTENTS

Notes from the Editor

Concrete poems are different from everyday poems; in fact, they're a lot more playful, as you might guess from the title of this book. What are they, you ask? Well, a concrete poem can be as simple as a single word, like "STOWAWAY" by Robert Carola. That word becomes a poem because of the unusual – and often humorous – way the type is placed on the page. A concrete poem can also be a selection of words arranged into a particular shape, like "Eskimo Pie" by John Hollander. The arrangement of letters or words on the page, the typefaces chosen and the way space is used add meaning to the poem beyond that contained in the actual words. Look at Robert Froman's "Easy Diver", for example, where the poem *is* the pigeon. Concrete poems, like Aram Saroyan's "Crickets", are often hard to read aloud, although sometimes they are irresistible: have a go at Helen Chasin's fourteen-line "Joy Sonnet in a Random Universe" – sh-boom, sh-boom! Finally, these visually arresting poems are accompanied by Chris Raschka's stunning illustrations, which have a poetry all of their own. Now turn the page for a dazzling, bewitching tour of thirty concrete poems from some of the world's finest visual poets and prepare for A POKE IN THE I.

Robert Froman

A SEEING POEM HAPPENS WHEN WORDS TAKE A SHAPE THAT HELPS THEM TO TURN ON A LIGHT IN SOMEONE'S MIND

go

ng!

A WEAK POEM

(To be read lying down)
Roger McGough

Oh dear, this poem is very weak

It can hardly stand up straight

Which comes from eating junk food

And going to bed too late.

4

a poem moves down a page

faster than a novel

Pigeon on the roof.

Dives.

Go-

ing

fa-

st.

G O I N G   T O

HIT HARD!

Opens   wings.

Softly,   gently,

down.

s
m
i
t
t
e
n
·
b
i
t
t
e
n

STOWAWAY

Robert Carola

eyeleveleye

Ronald Johnson

I
NEED
CONTACT

L E N S E S

like I need a poke in the eye

John Hegley

SKIPPING ROPE SPELL
John Agard

Turn rope turn, Don't trip my feet, For my skipping feet, Turn rope turn, Turn rope turn,

Turn rope turn, Turn round and round, Turn in the air, Turn on the ground.

Turn rope turn, Turn to the north, Turn to the south, But please rope, please, Don't make me out.

One for your high, One for your low, Turn rope turn, Not too fast, Not too slow.

13

QUEUE

Sylvia Cassedy

The
life
of
this
queue
depends
only
on
you.
One
step
out
of
line

and
it
all
breaks
in
two.

M
E
R
G
A F
T R
IFNIGC

Allen Jones

ESKIMO PIE

John Hollander

I shall
never pretend
to have forgotten
such loves as those
that turned the dying
brightness at an end of
a childs afternoon into
preludes To an evening of
lamplight To a night dark
with blanketing To mornings
of more and more There deep
in the old ruralities of play
the frosted block with papery
whisps still stuck to it kissed
me burningly as it arose out of
dry icy stillnesses And there now
again I taste first its hard then
its soft Now I am into the creamy
treasure which to have tasted is to
have begun to lose to the heat of a
famished sun But O if I break faith
with you poor dreadful popsicle may
my mouth forget warm rains a tongue
must Pauillac cool skin all tastes

I see
sweet
drops
slide
along
a hot
stick
It is
a sad
sorry
taste
which
never
comes
to an
end

Popsicle
Popsicle
tickle
tongue fun
licksicle
sticksicle
please
don't run
dripsicle
slipsicle
melt, melt
tricky
stopsicle
plopsicle
hand all
sticky

17

NO PRETENDING
Robert Froman

DANDELION, BRIGHT DANDELION

You

are

not

for

any-

thing,

You

just

are.

she loves me

she loves me not

she loves

she loves me

she

she loves

she

SKY DAY DREAM

Robert Froman

WITH THEM

COULD FLY OFF

I WISHED THAT I

INTO THE SKY

FLY OFF

SOME CROWS

ONCE I SAW

```
crickets
crickess
cricksss
cricssss
crisssss
crssssss
csssssss
ssssssss
ssssssts
ssssssets
sssskets
ssscckets
ssickets
srickets
crickets
```

21

THE SALMON
Douglas Florian

Could do with legs!
Just think what we
Our pearly eggs.
Upstream we spawn
We somersault!
We vault!
We jump!
Our leaps astound!
We bound!
We spring!

You'll see a saw

Upon my jaw,

But I can't cut

A two-by-four,

Or build a bed,

Or frame a door.

My splendid saw's

For goring fishes –

I eat them raw

And don't do dishes.

23

SWAN AND SHADOW

John Hollander

```
                    Dusk
                  Above the
              water hang the
                      loud
                      flies
                      Here
                    O so
                    gray
                    then
              What          A  pale signal will appear
              When          Soon before its shadow fades
              Where          Here in this pool of opened eye
              In us      No Upon us As at  the very edges
                of  where we take shape in the dark air
                this object  bares its  image awakening
                ripples of recognition that will
                brush darkness up into light
even after this bird this hour both drift by atop the perfect sad instant now
                already passing out of sight
                toward yet-untroubled reflection
              this image bears its object darkening
              into memorial shades Scattered bits of
              light         No of water Or something across
              water          Breaking up No Being regathered
              soon           Yet by then a swan will have
              gone               Yes out of mind into what
              vast
              pale
                hush
                of a
                place
                past
      sudden dark as
          if  a swan
              sang
```

FORSYTHIA

WHEE

Robert Froman

PACKED SNOW STEEP HILL FAST SLED

BALLOON

Colleen Thibaudeau

as
big as
ball as round
as sun . . . I tug
and pull you when
you run and when
wind blows I
say politely
HOLD
ME
TIGHTLY

GIRAFFE

Maureen W. Armour

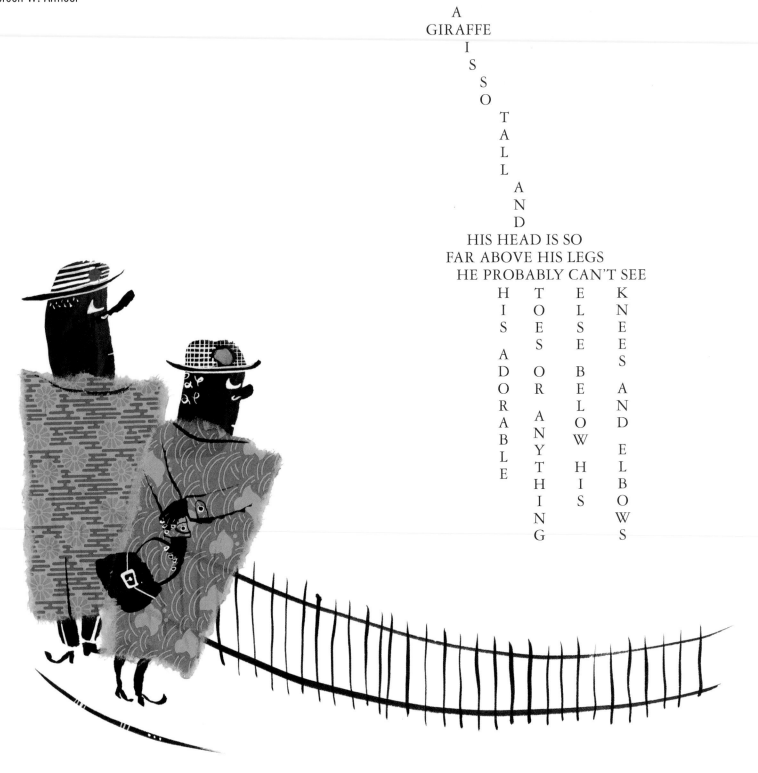

A
GIRAFFE
IS
SO
TALL
AND
HIS HEAD IS SO
FAR ABOVE HIS LEGS
HE PROBABLY CAN'T SEE

HIS ADORABLE

TOES OR ANYTHING

ELSE BELOW HIS

KNEES AND ELBOWS

a   a   a   a   a

   c   c   c   c

r   r   r   r   r

o   o   o   o

b   b   b   b   b

   a   a   a   a

t   t   t   t

s   s   s   s

t   t   t   t

   a   a   a   a

b   b   b   b   b

o   o   o   o

r   r   r   r   r

   c   c   c   c

a   a   a   a   a

Ian Hamilton Finlay

Tennis

game I

for hours

neck won't

is a

could watch

but my

let me

PATTERN POEM WITH
AN ELUSIVE INTRUDER

Reinhard Döhl

Sometimes I'm happy: la la la la la la
la la la la la la la la la la la la la la la
la la la la. Tum tum ti tum. La la la la la la
la la la la la la la la la la la la la la la la.
Hey nonny nonny. La la la la la la la la la
la la la la la la la la la la. Vo do di o do.
Poo poo pi doo. La la la la la la la la la la
la la la la la la la la la la la la la la la la
la la. Whack a doo. La la la la la la la. Sh-
boom, sh-boom. La la la la la la la la la
la la la la la la la la la la la la la la la la
la la. Dum di dum. La la la la la la la la
la la la la la la la la la. Tra la la. Tra la la
la la la la la la la la la la. Yeah yeah yeah.

ACKNOWLEDGEMENTS

"A Seeing Poem" by Robert Froman, from *Seeing Things* by Robert Froman, published by Thomas Y. Crowell, 1974. © 1974 Robert Froman. Reprinted by permission of Katherine Froman.

"Visual Soundpoem" by Edwin Morgan, from *Collected Poems* by Edwin Morgan, published by Carcanet Press Limited, Manchester, 1996. © 1971 Carcanet Press. Reprinted by permission of Carcanet Press Limited.

"A Weak Poem" from *Bad, Bad Cats* by Roger McGough. Reprinted by permission of PFD on behalf of Roger McGough. © 1997 Roger McGough.

"A Poem" by Richard Meltzer, from *The Kingfisher Book of Comic Verse,* Roger McGough, Ed., published by Kingfisher Press, 1986.

"Cat Chair" by Chris Raschka. © 2001 Chris Raschka.

"Easy Diver" by Robert Froman, from *Street Poems* by Robert Froman, published by McCall Publishing Co., 1971. © 1971 Robert Froman. Reprinted by permission of Katherine Froman.

"Snake Date" by Jean Balderston. First published in *Light: A Quarterly of Humorous, Occasional, Ephemeral and Light Verse,* 1993. Reprinted by permission of the author.

"I Need Contact Lenses" by John Hegley, from *The Kingfisher Book of Comic Verse,* Roger McGough, Ed., published by Kingfisher Press, 1986.

"Eyelevel" by Ronald Johnson, from *Concrete Poetry: A World View,* Mary Ellen Solt, Ed., published by Indiana University Press, 1970. Reprinted by permission of Indiana University Press.

"Skipping Rope Spell" by John Agard from *No Hickory, No Dickory, No Dock,* published by Penguin 1991. Reprinted by kind permission of John Agard c/o Caroline Sheldon Literary Agency.

"Queue" by Sylvia Cassedy, from *Zoomrimes: Poems About Things That Go,* published by HarperCollins, 1993. © 1993 the Estate of Sylvia Cassedy. Reprinted by permission of Ellen Cassedy.

"The Salmon" and "The Sawfish" by Douglas Florian, from *In the Swim.* © 1997 Douglas Florian. Reprinted by permission of Harcourt, Inc.

"Eskimo Pie" by John Hollander, from *Types of Shape* by John Hollander, published by Yale University Press, 1991. © 1991 Yale University Press. Reprinted by permission of Yale University Press.

"Popsicle" from *Splish Splash.* Text © 1994 Joan Bransfield Graham. Reprinted by permission of Houghton Mifflin/Ticknor & Fields Books for Young Readers. All Rights reserved.

"No Pretending" by Robert Froman, from *Street Poems* by Robert Froman, published by McCall Publishing Co., 1971. © 1971 Robert Froman. Reprinted by permission of Katherine Froman.

"She Loves Me" by Emmett Williams, from *Speaking Pictures: A Gallery of Pictorial Poetry from the Sixteenth Century to the Present*, Milton Klonsky, Ed., published by Harmony Books, 1975.

"Sky Day Dream" by Robert Froman, from *Seeing Things* by Robert Froman, published by Thomas Y. Crowell, 1974. © 1974 Robert Froman. Reprinted by permission of Katherine Froman.

"Crickets" by Aram Saroyan, from *Concrete Poetry: A World View*, Mary Ellen Solt, Ed., published by Indiana University Press, 1970. Reprinted by permission of Indiana University Press.

"Swan and Shadow" by John Hollander, first published in *Poetry* magazine, 1966. © 1966 Modern Poetry Association. Reprinted by permission of the Editor of *Poetry*.

"Forsythia" by Mary Ellen Solt, from *Concrete Poetry: A World View*, Mary Ellen Solt, Ed., published by Indiana University Press, 1970. Reprinted by permission of Indiana University Press.

"Whee" by Robert Froman, from *Seeing Things* by Robert Froman, published by Thomas Y. Crowell, 1974. © 1974 Robert Froman. Reprinted by permission of Katherine Froman.

"Balloon" by Colleen Thibaudeau. Reprinted by permission of Colleen Thibaudeau.

"Giraffe" by Maureen W. Armour. Reprinted by permission of Maureen W. Armour.

"Acrobats" by Ian Hamilton Finlay, from *An Anthology of Concrete Poems*, Emmett Williams, Ed., published by Something Else Press, 1967. © 1967 Ian Hamilton Finlay.

"Tennis Anyone?" by Monica Kulling. © 2001 Monica Kulling. Reprinted by permission of Marian Reiner for the author.

"Pattern Poem with an Elusive Intruder" by Reinhard Döhl, from *An Anthology of Concrete Poems*, Emmett Williams, Ed., published by Something Else Press, 1967. © 1967 Reinhard Döhl.

While every effort has been made to obtain permission to reprint copyright material, there may be cases where we have been unable to trace a copyright holder. The publisher will be happy to correct any omission in future printings.

la la la Ya

oo. La la la la l

n. La la la la l

la la la la la l

m. La la la la l

a la la. Tra l

a la la la Ye

la la la la la la

la la la. Sh-

la la la la la la

la la la la la

la. Tra la la la

h yeah yeah

PAUL B. JANECZKO is a poet and teacher and has edited more than twenty award-winning poetry anthologies for young people, including *Seeing the Blue Between: Advice and Inspiration for Young Poets*, and *A Kick in the Head: An Everyday Guide to Poetic Forms*. He says, "I want young readers to see the spectacular possibilities of poetry. I'm hoping this 'poke in the I' kicks kids' imaginations into high gear and lets them run wild writing their own concrete poems." Paul B. Janeczko lives in Maine, USA with his wife and daughter.

CHRIS RASCHKA is the illustrator of many highly praised books for children, including *I Pledge Allegiance* by Bill Martin Jr and Michael Sampson, *Yo! Yes?*, a Caldecott Honor Book; *Charlie Parker Played Be Bop*; *Arlene Sardine*; *A Child's Christmas in Wales* and *A Kick in the Head*. He says, "Concrete poetry is the yoga of words. Like feeling your breath and your bones, you begin to notice what words and sentences actually look like. It's just like the feeling you get after a fifteen-minute headstand. And you don't even have to put on loose-fitting clothes!" Chris Raschka lives in New York City, USA with his wife and son.